THOUGHT RELICS

LECTOR HOUSE PUBLIC DOMAIN WORKS

THOUGHT RELICS

RABINDRANATH TAGORE

ISBN: 978-93-5420-126-4

Published: 1921

LECTOR HOUSE LLP
E-MAIL: lectorpublishing@gmail.com

THOUGHT RELICS

BY

RABINDRANATH TAGORE

AUTHOR OF "GITANJALI," "THE GARDENER,"
"FRUIT GATHERING," ETC.

THOUGHT RELICS

L AST night I dreamt that I was the same boy that I had been before my mother died. She sat in a room in a garden house on the bank of the Ganges. I carelessly passed by without paying attention to her, when all of a sudden it flashed through my mind with an unutterable longing that my mother was there. At once I stopped and went back to her and bowing low touched her feet with my head. She held my hand, looked into my face, and said: "You have come!"

In this great world we carelessly pass by the room where Mother sits. Her storeroom is open when we want our food, our bed is ready when we must sleep. Only that touch and that voice are wanting. We are moving about, but never coming close to the personal presence, to be held by the hand and greeted: "You have come!"

I N my early years, I did not know that my sight had become impaired. The first day when, by chance, I put on a pair of eye-glasses I found that I had suddenly come nearer to everything. I felt I had gained the world twice as much as had been given to me the moment before.

There is such a thing as coming to the nearer presence of the world through the soul. It is like a real home-coming into this world. It is gaining the world more than can be measured--like gaining an instrument, not merely by having it, but by producing upon it music.

S PIRITUAL life is the emancipation of consciousness. Through it we find immediate response of soul everywhere. Before we attain this life, we see men through the medium of self-interest, prejudice or classification, because of the perpetual remoteness around us which we cannot cross over. When the veil is removed, we not only see the fleeting forms of the world, but come close to its eternal being, which is ineffable beauty.

Some seek for the evidence of spiritual truth in the outside world. In this quest one may stumble upon ghosts or some super-sensual phenomenon of nature, but these do not lead us to spiritual truth, as new words in a dictionary do not give us literature.

T O-DAY is the special day of the yearly festival of our *asram*, and we must make time to realise in the heart of this place the truth which is beauty.

And for this we have lighted our lamps. In the morning, the sun came out brightly; in the dusk the stars held up their lights. But these were not sufficient for us. Until we light our own little lamps, the world of lights in the sky is in vain, and unless we make our own preparations, the great wealth of the world preparations remains waiting like a lute for the finger touch.

INEED have no anxiety about the world of nature. The sun does not wait to be trimmed by me.

But from the early morning all my thoughts are occupied by this little world of my self. Its importance is owing to the fact that I have a world given to me which is mine. It is great because I have the power to make it worthy of its relationship with me; it is great, because by its help I can offer my own hospitality to the God of all the world.

IN our everyday world we live in poverty; our resources have to be husbanded with care; our strength becomes exhausted, and we come to our God as beggars for our joy of life. On festival days, we display our wealth and say to Him that we are even as He is; and we are not afraid to spend. This is the day when we bring to Him our own gift of joy. For we truly meet God, when we come to Him with our offerings and not with our wants.

LIFE'S highest opportunity is to be able to offer hospitality to our God. We live in God's world and forget Him, for the blind acceptance which is one-sided never finds its truth. It is a desert which receives rain but never offers fruit in return and its receiving has no meaning. God's world is given to us and when we offer our world to God then the gift is realised.

WHEN I had thrust the great world unnoticed behind the bars of my office habit I developed in me the belief that I was indispensable. Of the many means by which Nature exacts work from man, this pride is one of the most efficient. Those who work for money, work only to the extent of their wages, up to a definite point, beyond which they would count it a loss to work. But those whose pride impels them to work, they have no rest; even over-time work is not felt as a loss by them.

So busy used I to be under the belief that I was indispensable, that I hardly dared to wink. My doctor now and again would warn me, saying: "Stop, take it easy." But I would reply: "How will things go on if I stop?" Just then my health failed me, the wheels of my car broke down and it came to a stop beneath this window. From here I looked out upon the limitless space. There I saw whirling the numberless flashing wheels of the triumphal chariot of time,--no dust raised, no din, not even a scratch left on the roadway. On a sudden I came to myself. I clearly perceived that things could get along without me. There was no sign that those wheels would stop, or drag the least bit, for lack of anyone in particular.

But is this to be admitted so easily as all that! Even if I admit it in words, my mind refuses assent. If it be really quite the same whether I go or stay, how then did my pride of self find a place in the universe, even for a moment? On what could it have taken its stand? Amidst all the plentifulness with which space and time are teeming, it was nevertheless not possible to leave out this self of mine. The fact that I am indispensable is proved by the fact that *I am*.

EGOISM is the price paid for the fact of existence. So long as I realise this price within me, so long do I steadfastly bear all the pains and penalties of keeping myself in existence. That is why the Buddhists have it, that to destroy egoism is to cut at the root of existence: for, without the pride of self it ceases to be worth while to exist.

However that may be, this price has been furnished from some fund or other,--in other words, it matters somewhere that I should be, and the price paid is the measure of how much it matters. The whole universe--every molecule and atom of it--is assisting this desire that I should be. And it is the glory of this desire which is manifest in my pride of self. By virtue of this glory this infinitesimal "I" is not lower than any other thing in this Universe, in measure or value.

MAN has viewed the desire in him to be in two different ways. Some have held it to be an impulse of Creative Power, some a joyous self-expression of Creative Love. And man sets before himself different goals as the object of his life according as he views the fact of his *being* as the revealment of Force or of Love.

The value which our entity receives from Power is quite different in its aspect from that which it receives from Love. The direction in which we are impelled by our pride, in the field of power, is the opposite of that given by our pride, in the field of Love.

POWER can be measured. Its volume, its weight, its momentum can all be brought within the purview of mathematics. So it is the endeavour of those who hold power to be supreme, to increase in bulk. They would repeatedly multiply numbers,--the number of men, the number of coins, the number of appliances. When they strive for success they sacrifice others' wealth, others' rights, others' lives; for sacrifice is the essence of the cult of Power; and the earth is running red with the blood of that sacrifice.

The distinctive feature of materialism is the measurability of its outward expression, which is the same thing as the finiteness of its boundaries. And the disputes, civil and criminal, which have raged in the history of man, have mostly been over these same boundaries. To increase one's own bounds one has necessarily to encroach upon those of others. So, because the pride of Power is the pride of quantity, the most powerful telescope, when pointed in the direction of Power, fails to reveal the shore of peace across the sea of blood.

BUT when engaged in adding up the quantities of these forces and facts of power, we do not find them to be an ever-increasing series. In our pursuit of the principle of accumulation we are all of a sudden held up by stumbling upon the principle of check which bars the way. We discover that there is not only onward motion, but there are also pauses. And we repeatedly find in history that whenever the blindness of Power has tried to overrule this rule of rhythm, it has committed suicide. And that is why man still remembers the story of the toppling over of the tower of Babylon.

So we see that the principle of Power, of which the outward expression is bulk, is neither the final nor the supreme Truth. It has to stop itself to keep time with the rhythm of the universe. Restraint is the gateway of the Good. The value of the Good is not measured in terms of dimension or multitude. He who has known it within himself feels no shame in rags and tatters. He rolls his crown in the dust and marches out on the open road.

WHEN from the principle of Power we arrive at the principle of Beauty, we at once understand that, all this while, we had been offering incense at the wrong shrine; that Power grows bloated on the blood of its victims only to perish of surfeit; that try as we may by adding to armies and armaments, by increasing the number and variety of naval craft, by heaping up our share of the loot of war, arithmetic will never serve to make true that which is untrue; that at the end we shall die crushed under the weight of our multiplication of things.

When the *Rishi, Yajnavalkya,* on the eve of his departure, offered to leave his wife *Maitreyi* well-established upon an enumeration of what he had gathered together during his life, she exclaimed:

What am I to do with these, which are not of the immortal spirit?

Of what avail is it to add and add and add? By going on increasing the volume of pitch of sound we can get nothing but a shriek. We can gain music only by restraining the sound and giving it the melody of the rhythm of perfection.

Man grows gigantic by the appropriation of everything for himself: he attains harmony by giving himself up. In this harmony is peace,--never the outcome of external organization or of coalition between power and power,--the peace which rests on truth and consists in curbing of greed, in the forgiveness of sympathy.

THE question is: "In which Truth is my entity to realise its fullest value,--in Power or in Love?" If we accept Power as that truth we must also recognise conflict as inevitable and eternal. According to many European writers the Religion of Peace and Love is but a precarious coat of armour within which the weak seek shelter, but for which the laws of nature have but scant respect. That which the timid preachers of religion anathematise as unrighteousness,--that alone is the sure road which leads man to success.

The opposite school do not wholly deny this. They admit the premises but they say:

Adharmēnaidhatē tābat, tato bhadrāni pashyati, tatah sapatnān jayati,--samūlastu vinashyati.

In unrighteousness they prosper, in it they find their good, through it they defeat their enemies,--but they perish at the root.

IT is still dark. The day is about to dawn. The stall-keepers, who gathered for the festival fair, have spent the winter night singing round the lighted fires. Now they are preparing to disperse. Their noise, unlike the birds' notes, disturbs the morning peace.

For man stands at the parting of the ways. His strings have to be tuned for a deeper and a more complex music than those of nature. Man has his mind which reasons, and his will which seeks its own path. These have not yet found their full harmony with their surroundings. Therefore they are apt to break out in the ugliness of discord.

But in this very ugliness lies the great hope of the future. For these discords are not mere facts which we are compelled to acknowledge; they are ugly facts. This itself asserts every moment, that they are not what they should be; they are incomplete, and they are hopeful because they are painful.

WE are like a stray line of a poem, which ever feels that it rhymes with another line and must find it, or miss its own fulfilment. This quest of the unattained is the great impulse in man which brings forth all his best creations. Man seems deeply to be aware of a separation at the root of his being, he cries to be led across it to a union; and somehow he knows that it is love which can lead him to a love which is final.

I HAVE a relationship with the world which is deeply personal. It is not of mere knowledge and use. All our relationships with facts have an infinite medium which is Law, *Satyam*; all our relationship with truth has an infinite medium which is Reason, *gnānam*; all our personal relationship has an infinite medium, which is Love, *ānandam*.

We are not mere facts in this world, like pieces of stones; we are persons. And therefore we cannot be content with drifting along the stream of circumstances. We have a central ideal of love with which to harmonise our existence, we have to manifest a truth in our life, which is the perfect relationship with the Eternal Person.

LAST night when the north wind was keen, like a sharp blade of steel, the stall-keepers improvised some kind of shelter with twigs and leaves. With all its flimsiness it was the most important necessity for them, for the time. But this morning, before it is light, we hear them shouting for their bullocks and dragging out from underneath the trees their creaking carts. It is urgently important for them now to leave their shelter.

"I want" has its constant counterweight--"I do not want." Otherwise the monster necessity, with its immovable weight, would crush all existence. For the moment we may sigh at the fact that nothing remains for long, but we are saved from permanent despair at the calamity that nothing moves at all. Things remain and things move--between these two contrary currents we have found our dwelling-place and freedom.

THE horse harnessed to a carriage is only a part of it, the master is he who drives it unattached. We are enjoined to work with vigour and yet retain our detachment of mind. For our deeds must express our freedom above all, otherwise we become like wheels revolving because compelled. There is a harmony between doing and not doing, between gaining and renouncing which we must attain.

Our daily flow of prayer carries our self into the supreme Self, it makes us feel the reality of that fulness which we gain by utterly giving ourselves up, makes our consciousness expand in a large world of peace, where movements are beauty and all relations are truths because of their inner freedom, which is disinterestedness.

OUR will attains its perfection when it is one with love, for only love is true freedom. This freedom is not in the negation of restraint. It spontaneously accepts bondage, because bondage does not bind it, but only measures its truth. Non-slavery is in the cessation of service, but freedom is in service itself.

A village poet of Bengal says:

> "In love the end is neither pain nor pleasure, but love only.
> Love gives freedom while it binds, for love is what unites."

LOVE is not a mere impulse, it must contain truth, which is law. It accepts limitations from truth because of its own inner wealth. The child willingly exercises restraint to correct its bodily balance, because it has true pleasure in the freedom of its movements; and love also counts no cost as too great to realise its truth. Poetry is much more strict in its form of expression than prose, because poetry has the freedom of joy in its origin and end. Our love of God is accurately careful of its responsibilities. It is austere in its probity and it must have intellect for its ally. Since what it deals with is immense in value, it has to be cautious about the purity of its coins. Therefore, when our soul cries for the gift of immortality, its first prayer is,--"Lead me from the unreal to Truth."

THE Father is working in his world, but the Beloved is lying asleep in our heart, in the depth of its darkness. He will wake only when our own love wakes. It may sound paradoxical to say that we are unconscious of our own love, as we are unconscious of the fact that the earth is carrying us round the sun. But the truth is that all parts of our nature are not fully illuminated, and in most cases we have the immediate knowledge of ourselves only on the surface where our mind is occupied with the temporary needs and ferments of our life.

TO wake up in love is not to wake up in a world of sweetness, but in the world of heroic endeavours where life wins its eternity through death, and joy its worth in suffering. As the most positive affirmation of truth is in love, it must realise itself through all that threatens us with deprivation. Poverty is afraid of the smallest loss, and wealth is daring in its expenditure. Love is the wealth of soul and therefore it reveals itself in utmost bravery and fortitude. And because it finds its resource in itself it begs not praise from men and no punishment can reach it from outside.

THE world of things in which we live misses its equilibrium when its communication with the world of love is lost. Then we have to pay with our soul for objects which are immensely cheap. And this can only happen when the prison walls of things threaten us with being final in themselves. Then it gives rise to terrible fights, jealousies and coercions, to a scramble for space and opportunities, for these are limited. We become painfully aware of the evil of this and try all measure of adjustment within the narrow bounds of a mutilated truth. This leads to failures. Only he helps us who proves by his life that we have a soul whose dwelling is in the kingdom of love, and things lose the tyranny of fictitious price when we come to our spiritual freedom.

IT is hard for us to free ourselves from the grip of our acquisitions. For the pull of their gravitation is towards the centre of our self. The force of perfect love acts towards the contrary direction. And this is why love gives us freedom from the weight of things. Therefore our days of joy are our days of expenditure. It is not the lightness of pressure in the outside world which we need in order to be free, but love which has the power to bear the world's weight, not only with ease, but with joy.

ONLY because we have closed our path to the inner world of freedom, has the outer world become terrible in its exactions. It is slavery to continue to live in a sphere where things are, yet their meaning is obstructed. It has become possible for men to say that existence is evil only because, in our blindness, we have missed something in which our existence has its truth. If a bird tries to soar in the sky with only one of its wings, it is offended with the wind for buffeting it down to the dust. All broken truths are evil. They hurt, because they suggest something which they do not offer. Death does not hurt us, but disease does, because disease constantly reminds us of health and yet withholds it from us. And life in a half world is evil, because it feigns finality when it is obviously incomplete, giving us the cup but not the draught of life.

COMING to the theatre of life we foolishly sit with our back to the stage. We see the gilded pillars and decorations, we watch the coming and going of the crowd; and when the light is put out at the end, we ask ourselves in bewilderment, what is the meaning of it all? If we paid attention to the inner stage, we could witness the eternal love drama of the soul and be assured that it has pauses, but no end, and that the gorgeous world-preparations are not a magnificent delirium of things.

WE criticise Nature from outside when we separate it in our mind from human nature, and blame it for being devoid of pity and justice. Let the wick burn with indignation at the want of light in the rest of the candle, but the truth is that the wick represents the whole candle in its illumination. Obstacles are necessary companions to expression, and we know that the positive element in language is not in its obstructiveness. Exclusively viewed from the side of the obstacle, Nature appears as inimical to the idea of morality. But if that were absolutely true, moral life could never come to exist. Life, moral or physical, is not a completed fact, but is a continual process, depending for its movement upon two contrary forces, the force of resistance and that of expression. Dividing these forces into two mutually opposing principles does not help us, for the truth dwells not in the opposition but in its continual reconciliation.

GOOD taste which is needful for the true understanding of a poem, comes from the vision of unity seen in the light of imagination. Faith has the similar function in our acceptance of life. It is a spiritual organ of sight which enables us instinctively to realise the vision of wholeness when in fact we only see the parts. Sceptics may scoff at this vision as an hallucination, they may select and arrange facts in such a manner as to disprove it and yet faith never doubts its own direct apprehension of the inner truth which binds, which builds, which heals, which leads to an ideal of fullness. Faith is this spontaneous response in our being to the voice of the all-pervading Yes, and therefore it is the greatest of all creative forces in human life. It is not merely a passive acknowledgment of truth, it is an ever active effort for attaining harmony with that peace which is in the rhythm of truth in creation, goodness which is in the rhythm of combination in society, and unity of love which is in the rhythm of self-realisation in soul. The mere fact of innumerable breaks in such a rhythm no more proves its unreality to a man gifted with faith than the prevalent fact of harsh notes and noises disproves the truth of music to a musician. It only calls him to a strenuous endeavour to mend the break and establish harmony with truth.

THE day breaks in the east, like a bud bursting its sheath to come out in flower. But if this fact belonged only to the outside world of events, however could we find our entrance into it? It is a sunrise in the sky of our consciousness, it is a new creation, fresh in bloom, in our life.

Open your eyes and see. Feel this world as a living flute might feel the breath of music passing through it, feel the meeting of creative joy in the depth of your consciousness. Meet this morning light in the majesty of your existence, where it is one with you. But if you sit with your face turned away, you build a separating barrier in the undivided sphere of creation, where events and the creative consciousness meet.

DARKNESS is that which isolates our consciousness within our own self. It hides the great truth of our unity with the world, giving rise to doubt and contention. Groping in the dark, we stumble against objects to which we cling, believing them to be the only things we have. When light comes we slacken our hold, finding them to be mere parts of the all to which we are related. This is freedom--freedom from the isolation of self, from the isolation of things which impart fierce intensity to our sense of possession. Our God is that freedom, for He is Light, and in that light we find out truth, which is our perfect relationship with all.

FEAR assumes unlimited dimensions in the dark, because it is the shadow of the self which has lost its foothold in the all; the self which is a doubter, an unbeliever, which puts its emphasis upon negation, exaggerating detached facts into fearful distortions. In the light we find the harmony of things and know that our world is great and therefore we are great; we know that, with more and more extensive realisation of truth, conflicts will vanish, for existence itself is harmony.

IN Nature we find the presence of law in truth, and the presence of joy in beauty. It is urgently necessary for us to know truth, but we are free to ignore the presence of joy. It is not safe for our life to forget that it becomes light in the morning; but we can safely forget that morning is beautiful, and yet live.

In this realm of truth we are bound, in the realm of beauty we are free. We must pay our homage to God where He rules; but we may laugh at Him where He loves. He keeps us bound where He binds Himself, He gives us freedom where He is infinite. The great power of beauty is in its modesty. It makes way for the least of us, it waits in silence. It must have our all or nothing, therefore it never asks. It suffers meekly when it is refused, but it has its eternity.

AN acquaintance of mine has suddenly died and once again I come to know death, the tritest of all truisms in this world.

The moralist teaches us to know the world as unreal through the contemplation of death. But to make renunciation easy by calling the world names is neither true, nor brave. For that renunciation is no renunciation at all in which things have lost their value.

On the contrary, the world is so true, that death's wheel leaves no mark upon it. The untruth is in the belief that this self of ours for its own permanent use can rob this world of even a particle of its things. Death has its concern only with our self and not with this world. The world never loses an atom, it is our self which suffers.

THERE are men whose idea of life is static, who long for its continuation after death only because of their wish for permanence and not perfection; they love to imagine that the things to which they are accustomed will persist for ever. They completely identify themselves in their minds with their fixed surroundings and with whatever they have gathered, and to have to leave these is death for them. They forget that the true meaning of living is outliving, it is ever growing out of itself. The fruit clings to its stem, its skin clings to the pulp and the pulp to the seed so long as the fruit is immature, so long as it is not ready for its course of further life. Its outer covering and its inner core are not yet differentiated and it only proves its life by its strength of tenacity. But when the seed is ripe its hold upon its surrounding is loosened, its pulp attains fragrance, sweetness and detachment, and is dedicated to all who need it. Birds peck at it and it is not hurt, the storm plucks it and flings it to the dust and it is not destroyed. It proves its immortality by its renunciation.

IN Hindu scriptures this world is considered to be an egg. If that be true, then this egg must have for its content a living being whose fulfillment is to break through its shell into a freer existence.

While our world feeds us, gives us shelter, it encloses us all around. The limitedness of our narrow sensibility and range of thought build the shell of our world egg, within which our consciousness is confined. If we could widen its boundaries even by a small fraction, if some of the invisible rays could come within our sphere of perception, if few more of the dance rhythms of creation could find response in some added strings of our senses, then the whole aspect of our world would be completely changed.

To come out of the bounds of our sensibility and mental vision into a wider freedom is the meaning of our immortality. Can we imagine in our present stage of confinement what that sphere of freedom is like? From the data of all the facts within the shell can a chick ever form the idea of the world to which it is to be born?

THE passivity which is the predominant fact of the shell life is secretly contradicted by the rudimentary wings. Likewise in the confinement of our present state, in spite of the fact that a great part of our life is passively obedient to circumstances, there struggles in us our aspiration for freedom against impediments that appear to be ultimate. This is our spiritual pair of wings which have their significance in a full opportunity to soar. Had immortality only meant an endless persistence of our shell itself then we should admit that these impotent wings were cursed by an evil power with an eternity of hindrance. But this we cannot admit. Man has ever talked of emancipation from what is present, from what seems final. While the spirit of life in him seeks continuance the spirit of immortality seeks emancipation.

THE life of the seed within the fruit is absolutely different from its life of growth as a tree. The life which is bound on all sides within the environment of our self, within the limited range of our senses must be so fundamentally different from the life of an emancipated soul that it is impossible to imagine the latter while we are immured in the sheath of self. And therefore in our desire for eternal life we pray for an eternity of our habit and comfort, forgetting that immortality is in repeatedly transcending the definite forms of life in order to pursue the infinite truth of life. Those who think that life's true meaning is in the persistence of its particular forms which are familiar to us are like misers who have not the power to know that the meaning of money can only be found by spending it, by changing the symbol into truth.

ALL our desires are but focussing our will to a limited range of experience. These become jealously tenacious and combative when we fail to imagine that our experience will widen. In our childhood we wished for an unbounded continuity in our enjoyment of a particular food or game and we refused to believe in the worth of a mature age which had different interests altogether. Those who build their vision of a life after death upon the foundation of desires belonging to the present life merely show their want of faith in Eternal life. They cling to what they have because they cannot believe that their love for the present is only an indication that this love will persist through their growth, stimulating it, and not that it will retard their growth altogether.

THE world of sleep is fundamental,--it is the world of the mother's womb. It is the world where the grass and the trees live and find their beauty of reposefulness. Our consciousness has freed itself from its embrace, asserting its independence. It is the freedom of the fountain which must come over and over again to its origin to renew its play. The whole depth and spread of the still water finds its own play in the play of this little fountain. In like manner, it is in our own consciousness that the universe knows itself. Therefore this consciousness has to be great in order to be true. Our consciousness is the music of the world, its dance, its poem. It has its pauses in the bosom of the original sleep, to be fed with immortality at her breast.

IN man's nature there is a division between the fleeting and the permanent, which the animals have not, because they live on the surface of life. Therefore they are saved from the danger of trying to give permanence to things which have not that quality in themselves. Only because man has to a great extent a preservative power in his inner world, does he try in his greed to keep his appetites ever fresh, steeping them in the elixir of imagination. These appetites are of outer nature, and for the animals they quit the stage when they have played their parts. But when we try to hoard them in our inner life we wrongly put upon them the seal of the infinite. Thus our land of immortality is every day being invaded by the retinue of death, and the servants who ought to be dismissed with their wages paid, are enshrined in our sanctuary.

WEALTH is the symbol of power. There-fore, wealth must move and flow in order to be perfect. For power is active, it is movement. But mere movement is superficial. It must be a growth and therefore continual gaining. This gain is something which not merely moves, but remains.

The highest harmony of movement and rest is in the spiritual life, whose essence is love. Love of God, nay, love in all forms, is the reaching of the goal and yet never coming to a stop. Power, when it reaches its end, stops and grows careful of its hoarding. Love, when it reaches its end, reaches endlessness and therefore is not afraid of spending its all.

BEING by nature social, some portion of our energies we must employ to keep up the flow of sociality. But its field and action are on the surface. The ripples of gregariousness are not the deep currents of human love. The men who have strong social instincts are not necessarily lovers of men.

The men who are spendthrifts very often lack true generosity. In most cases they cannot give, but can only spend. And also like them the social men can spend themselves, but not give themselves. This reckless spending creates a vacuum which we fill up with the débris of activities, whose object is to bury time.

BUT we cannot afford to fritter away our solitude where lies the throne of the infinite. We cannot truly live for one another, if we never claim the freedom to live alone, if our social duties consist in helping one another to forget that we have souls. To exhaust ourselves completely in mere efforts to give company to each other, is to cheat the world of our best, the best which is the product of the amplitude of our inner atmosphere of leisure. Society poisons the air it breathes, where it hems in the individual with a revolving crowd of distractions.

IN our country it is accounted the greatest calamity to have one's courtyard brought under the plough. Because, in the courtyard, man has made his very own the immense wealth called space. Space is not a rare commodity outside, but one does not *get* it till he can bring it inside and make it his own. The space of the courtyard, man has made part of his home. Here the light of the sun is revealed as his own light, and here his baby claps his little hands to call to the moon. So if the courtyard be not kept open, but be used for sowing crops, then is the nest destroyed in which the outside Universe can come and dwell as man's own universe.

THE difference between a really rich man and a poor man is, that the former can afford vast open spaces in his home. The furniture with which a rich man encumbers his house may be valuable, but the space with which he makes his courtyard wide, his garden extensive, is of infinitely greater value. The business place of the merchant is crowded with his stock,--there he has not the means of keeping spaces vacant, there he is miserly, and millionaire though he be, there he is poor. But in his home that same merchant flouts mere utility by the length and breadth and height of his room--to say nothing of the expanse of his garden--and gives to space the place of honour. It is here that the merchant is rich.

Not only unoccupied space, but unoccupied time, also, is of the highest value. The rich man out of his abundance, can purchase leisure. It is in fact a test of his riches, this power to keep fallow wide stretches of time, which want cannot compel him to plough up.

There is yet another place where an open expanse is the most valuable of all,--and that is in the mind. Thoughts which must be thought, from which there is no escape, are but worries. The thoughts of the poor and the miserable cling to their minds as the ivy to a ruined temple.

Pain closes up all openings of the mind. Health may be defined as the state in which the physical consciousness lies fallow, like an open heath. Let there be but a touch of gout in the remotest toe and the whole of consciousness is filled with pain, leaving not a corner empty.

Just as one cannot live grandly without unoccupied spaces, so the mind cannot think grandly without unoccupied leisure,--otherwise for it truth becomes petty. And like dim light, petty truth distorts vision, encourages fear, and keeps narrow the field of communion between man and man.

IN society, we find our places according to a certain conventional price set upon us, like toys arranged in the shop windows, according to their value. This makes us forget that we are not for sale, that the social man is not the whole man.

I have known a fisherman singing, while fishing all day in the Ganges, who was pointed out to me by my boatman with awe as a man possessed by God. He is out of reach of the fluctuation of market prices, for he has found out the infinite value of the soul which the monarchs of the world have not. In history there were men who are still recognized by their eternal worth; but this recognition is not the only proof of their value. For immortality is not in its outer manifestation, and dark rays are rays all the same, though we do not see them. The figure of this fisherman comes to my mind when I think that their number is not small who with their lives sing the epic of the freedom of soul, but will never be known in history.

OUR aspiration becomes easy when through us our community aspires. Money-making is pursued by most men, not merely because money is useful, but rather because it is desired by others. The savages' lust for head-hunting becomes irresistible when it is prevalent in the community. When the majority wishes through us, we are ready to sacrifice truth to its claims.

Doubts assail us and strength fails in our aspiration for spiritual life chiefly because it is not the aspiration of the surrounding crowd. Therefore our wish for the highest has to be so immensely true, so that it can sustain itself in all circumstances against the constant pressure of the crowd's wish. We need all the succour of the eternal to fight against the combined antagonism of the congregated moments.

OUR thoughts naturally move in their surrounding element of man's mind, like birds in the air. This sky of mind is perpetually troubled by contrary wind-currents, by doubts and denials, by levity and pride; it is obscured by the dust and smoke of the busy world. Our spiritual wings require spontaneity of speed, grace of perfect movement; but when they are constantly buffeted by noisy gusts from all sides it makes us too conscious of our limitations, and consequently that self-abandonment becomes difficult which is necessary for our communion with the Infinite. And yet the task has to be done and the most difficult path taken for the highest attainment of life. The great teachers have ever won that infinity of solitude needed for soul's meeting with her God, through the crowd and for the crowd themselves. In the lives of these men we witness the proof of our own limitless power, and the faith that we thus gain gives freedom to our aspiration in the face of adversity.

SOME part of the earth's water becomes rarefied and ascends to the skies. With the movement and the music it acquires in those pure heights it then showers down, back to the water of the earth, making it wholesome and fresh. Similarly, part of the mind of humanity rises up out of the world and flies skywards; but this sky-soaring mind attains completeness only when it has returned, to mingle with the earth-bound mind. This is the ventilation of religion, the circulation of man's ideals between heaven and earth.

THERE are the rain of mud, the rain of blood, and such like dire phenomena of which we hear tell. These happen when the purity of the atmosphere is sullied and the air is burdened with dirt. Then it is not the song of the sky which descends in purifying showers, but just the earth's own sins which fall back on it. Then our religion itself grows muddy, the collective egoism of the people assumes pious names, and we boast of our God taking the lead in our adventures of sell-seeking, in our campaign of hatred.

TO–DAY on the sin-laden dust of the earth pours tainted rain from the sky. Our long wait for the cleansing bath in pure water from on high has been repeatedly doomed to disappointment; the mud is soiling our minds and marks of blood are also showing. How long can we keep on wiping this away? Even the pure silence of the empyrean is powerless to clarify the discordant notes of the prayer for peace which is rising from a blood-stained world.

Peace? Who can truly pray for Peace? Only they who are ready to renounce.

Atha dheerā amrtatvam viditvā
Druvam adhruvēshviha na prārthayantē.

Men of tranquil mind, being sure of Immortal Truth, never seek the eternal in things of the moment.

OUR greatest men have shown immense respect for mankind in their expectations. We come to believe in ourselves because of what is asked of us. Practical men base their arrangements upon their estimates of man's limitations. Therefore the great creations of history, the creations that have their foundation upon the faith in the infinite in man, have not their origin in the common-sense of practical men. When Buddha said to men: "Spread thy thoughts of love beyond limits," when Christ said: "Love thine enemies," their words transcended the average standard of ideals belonging to the ordinary world. But they ever remind us that our true life is not the life of the ordinary world, and we have a fund of resources in us which is inexhaustible. It is not for us to despair, because the highest hope for mankind has been uttered by the great words of great men.

IT is an important duty for man so to bear himself that he may not fail to be recognized as man,--not only in his own interest, but because of his responsibilities to others. The man who belittles himself lowers not only his own value but that of all mankind. Man knows himself as great where he sees great men,--and the truer is such vision of greatness, the easier it becomes to be great.

TO fledgeling birds flight in the sky may appear incredible. They may with apparent reason measure the highest limit of their possibilities by the limited standard of their nests. But, in the meanwhile, they find that their food is not grown inside those nests, it is brought to them across the measureless blue. There is a silent voice that speaks to them, that they are more than what they are, and that they must not laugh at the message of soaring wings and glad songs of freedom.

THE more we feel afraid of pain, the more we build all kinds of hiding places in which to hide ourselves from our own truth. Our wealth and honour are barricades that keep us at arm's length from the touch of our own true selves. Thus we become more familiar with that which we have, than that which we are. Our sufferings seek us out through our protections; they take away our artificial props and set us face to face with our naked loneliness.

This stripping bare of our deeper selves is not only necessary for self-exploration and the discovery of our innermost resources, but it is also needed for our purification. For beneath our safe cover of prosperity and comfort, dirt and dead matter gather every day waiting to be cleared by the rude rubbing of pain.

THE old is prudent but is not wise. Wisdom is that freshness of mind which enables one to realise that truth is not hoarded in caskets of maxims, it is free and living. Great sufferings lead us to wisdom because these are the birth-throes through which our mind is freed from its habit-environment, and comes naked into the arms of reality. Wisdom has the character of the child perfected through knowledge and feeling.

MORNING has its birds' songs, and life's daybreak has the music of the child. At every home comes to us this refrain of life with its pure notes of beauty. The bloom constantly is brushed off the world of man by the friction of its dirt, it is roughened and begrimed by the callous touch of age; yet there flows unobstructed the daily renewal of humanity in its ceaseless rebirths. The eternal repeats its call at man's gate in every child, and the morning's message keeps its melody unimpaired.

It rouses response to-day in my heart, the life's awakening call that comes from the children's shouts and songs round me, and I feel that creation finds its own true voice in them, the creation which keeps nestled in its heart the spirit of the child.

THIS symphony made of the morning light and children's mirth does not speak to me of pure joy. For in my heart it mingles with another strain which tempers its sparkle with a shade of sadness. It is a cry of unattained harmony, unfulfilled hope. The simple notes of ideal completeness, dash themselves against life's complexities, rugged with flaws and fractures, and a sob of anguish spreads over our thoughts. For pain finds its own music in the notes that joy brings to it from heaven, as the pebbles find theirs from the flow of the laughing stream.

EXISTENCE is the play of the fountain of immortality. Wash your soul with its water, you who are old, and feel that you are of the same age with the flower that has blossomed this morning and with this light which carries fresh in its countenance the first smile of creation. This is freedom, freedom from the mist which for the time being masks our spirit with the semblance of blurred age, hiding from us the truth that we are the children of the immortal. Could the child bring such a joy to the heart of man if age and death were true? Does not that joy come from a direct recognition of the truth of deathless life, of endless growth and ever-renewed hope of perfection?

TO alleviate pain, to try to remove its causes, are worthy of man. All the same, we must know that a great part of our sufferings has to be ascribed to the beginning of our entrance into a new plane of existence to which our vital nature has not been completely adapted nor our mind thoroughly accustomed. From a narrow perfection of animality man has arrived in the imperfectness of spiritual life, where the civil war between the forces of our primitive past and those belonging to our future has robbed us of peace. Not having reached its normal stage humanity is enveloped in the incandescent vapour of suffering.

MAN'S greatness is like the morning sun, its horizon is far before us. Man truly lives in the life that is beyond him; he toils for the unknown master, he stores for the unborn, he leaves the best harvest of his life for reapers who have not yet come; the time which is yet to be is truer to him than the time which is. Man offers himself as a sacrifice for all that lies in future; the motive power which guides the course of his growth is expectation. All this shows that man is not yet born, his history is the history of birth-throes. Our greatest men bring in their life the message of man's future birth; for they dwell in the time to come, making it ready for ourselves. They reveal to us a life whose glory is not in the absence of suffering, but in the fact that its sufferings have been made creative, transmuted into the stuff of life itself. It is like the tree which garners the sun's heat and light in its fibre and breaks out in beauty of fruitfulness. By extinguishing the fire of pain man may find his comfort, his period of slumber, which is the period of stagnant time, an imprisoned present; but by mastering this fire he lights his lamp of wisdom which gives illumination to the endless future.

THERE are sufferings about which the question comes to our mind whether we deserve them. We must frankly acknowledge that explanations are not offered to us. So it does not help us in the least to complain, let us rather be worthy of the challenge thrown to us by them. That we have been wounded is a fact which can be ignored, but that we have been brave is a truth of the highest importance. For the former belongs to the outer world of cause and effect, while the latter belongs to the world of spirit.

WE must know that to be provided with an exact apportionment of what we deserve and need, is like travelling in a world whose flatness is ideally perfect, and therefore where the fluid forces of nature are held in suspense. We require ups and downs, however unpleasant they may be, in our life's geography, in order to make our thoughts and energies fluently active. Our life's journey is a journey in an unknown country, where hills and hollows come in our way unawares, keeping our minds ever active in dealing with them. They do not come according to our deserts, but our deserts are judged according to our treatment of them.

WHEN the ship's hold is full of water then only does the buffeting of the outside waters become a menace. The inside water is not so visibly threatening, its tumult not so stupendously apparent,--it destroys with its dead weight. So the temptation is strong to cast all the blame on the waves outside. But if good sense does not dawn in time, of all hands manning the pumps, then sinking is inevitable. However hopeless the task of getting rid of the internal water may now and then appear, it is surely more hopeful than trying to bale away the water of the outside seas!

Obstacles and opposition from without there always will be, but they become dangers only when there are also obstacles and opposition within.

WHEN we come to believe that we are in possession of our God because we belong to some particular sect it gives us such a complete sense of comfort, that God is needed no longer except for quarrelling with others whose idea of God differs from ours in theoretical details.

Having been able to make provision for our God in some shadow-land of creed we feel free to reserve all the space for ourselves in the world of reality, ridding it of the wonder of the infinite, making it as trivial as our own household furniture. Such unlimited vulgarity only becomes possible when we have no doubt in our minds that we believe in God while our life ignores Him.

THE pious man of sect is proud because he is confident of his right of possession in God. The man of devotion is meek because he is conscious of God's right of love over his life and soul. The object of our possession becomes smaller than ourselves, and without acknowledging it in so many words the bigoted sectarian has an implicit belief that God can be kept secured for certain individuals in a cage which is of their own make. In a similar manner the primitive races of men believe that their ceremonials have a magic influence upon their deities. Sectarianism is a perverse form of worldliness in the disguise of religion; it breeds a narrowness of heart in a greater measure than the cult of the world based upon material interest can ever do. For undisguised pursuit of self has its safety in its openness, like filth exposed to the sun and air. But the self-magnification with its consequent lessening of God that goes on unchecked under the cover of sectarianism loses its chance of salvation because it defiles the very source of purity.

RELIGION, like poetry, is not a mere idea, it is expression. The self-expression of God is in the endless variedness of creation; and our attitude towards the Infinite Being must also in its expression have a variedness of individuality ceaseless and unending. Those sects which jealously build their boundaries with too rigid creeds excluding all spontaneous movement of the living spirit may keep hoarded their theology but they kill religion.

THE attempt to make the one religion which is their own prevail for all time and space, comes naturally to men addicted to sectarianism. This makes it offensive to them to be told that God is generous in his distribution of love, and his means of communication with men have not been restricted to a blind lane abruptly stopping at one historical point of time and place. If humanity ever happens to be overwhelmed with a catastrophe of a universal flood of one religion then God will have to make provision for another Noah's Ark to save his creatures from a spiritual destruction.

WHEN religion is in the complete possession of the sect and is made smooth to the level of the monotonous average, it becomes correct and comfortable, but loses the living spirit of art. For art is the expression of the universal through the individual, and religion in its outer aspect is the art of the human soul. It almost becomes a matter of pride and a sign of superior culture to be able to outrage all codes of decency imposed by an authorised religion bearing the stamp of approval of an organisation which can persecute but has not the power to persuade.

As an analogous phenomenon, we have known literary men deliberately cultivating a dread of whatever has the reputation of goodness, and also men of art afraid of being suspected as a lover of the beautiful. They rebel against the fact that what is proper and what is true in beauty and in goodness have become mixed up in men's mind. The appraisement of what is proper does not require any degree of culture or natural sensitiveness of mind, and therefore it fetches a ready price in the market, outbids truth, becomes petty in its tyranny and leaves smudges of vulgarity upon things that are precious. To rescue truth from the dungeon of propriety has ever been the mission, of poets and artists, but in the time of revolution they are apt to go further by rejecting truth itself.

In our epic Rāmāyana we find that when Prince Rāmachandra won back his wife from the clutches of the giant who had abducted her, his people clamoured for her rejection, suspecting defilement. Similarly in art fastidious men of culture are clamouring for the banishment of the beautiful because she has been allowed to remain so long in the possession of propriety.

THOSE who have their enterprises in the world of nature, master her forces, becoming rich in wealth and power. The greatest gain which comes across their path in their adventures is moral truth. For power is combination, and all combinations, in order to be perfect, need the help of the moral law, in which individuals acknowledge the universal principle of the good. Moral truth is most needed when men move, and move together.

But laws, whether in nature where it is physical, or in society where it is moral, are external. They are formal, lacking that deeper mystery of perfectness, which is creation; which is in the beauty of harmony in nature; which is in the beauty of love in man. Law is the channel of finitude through which things evolve without ceasing, but its meaning lies in its revolution round an inner centre which is infinite. We follow law to live; we reach the centre to find immortality.

FOLLOWING the interminable current of law, exploring the countless fields of forces and openings of wealth, we talk of endless endeavour but of no ultimate gain. We know that power thrives in moving. When it stumble against some final object it receives its death fall. We of all peoples in the world know to our cost that when nations grow weary of their quest, settling down to store up and to arrange their possessions; when with their distrust of new ideas their morals stiffen into conventions, becoming unfit to guide them in the path of life's adventures, keeping them bound to growthless traditions, then they are gradually pushed away from life's high road by the moving forces of history.

But this endlessness of movement in the outer world only proves that there we have no goal to reach and our goal is somewhere else. It is in the inner region of spirit. There our deepest longing is for that peace which rests upon fulfilment. There we meet our God. He is the ever-moving power in the world. He is the ever-reposing love in the soul. God eludes us in nature to call us onward; in the soul He surrenders Himself to gather us to His heart. This is why, in the realm of power, we grow by aggrandisement; but, in the realm of love we grow by renunciation. This is why though in our worldly ambition pride acts as an incentive, it is the greatest of all obstacles in our spiritual aspiration.

IN a lyrical poem, the metre and the idea are blended in one. Treated separately, they reveal themselves as two contrary forces; and instances are common in which their natural antagonism has not been overcome, thus resulting in the production of bad poems.

We are the artists, before whom lie materials which are mutually obstructive. They continually clash, until they develop into a creation perfect in unity. Very often, in order to shirk trouble and secure peace, we sacrifice one of the contending parties. This makes the fight impossible, but also the creation. The restless spirit of nature divorced from the soul's repose drives us to the madness of work which piles up towers of things. On the other hand the spiritual being deprived of its world of reality lives only in the exile of abstraction, creating phantoms in which exaggerations, unchecked by the strict necessities of forms, run riot.

WHEN the man-made world is less an expression of man's creative soul than a mechanical device for some purposes of power, then it hardens and narrows itself, attains too definite a character, leading to proficiency at the cost of the immense suggestiveness of life. In his creative activities man establishes human relationships with his surroundings, making nature instinct with his own life and love. But with his utilitarian energies he fights nature, banishes her from his world, deforms and defiles her with the ugliness of his callous ambitions. This world of man's own manufacture with its discordant shrieks and mechanical movements incessantly suggests to him and convinces him of a scheme of universe which is an abstract system and which has no touch of the person and therefore no ultimate reality.

WITH the truth of our expression we grow in truth. The truth of art is in the disinterested joy of creation, which is fatally injured when betrayed into a purpose alien to itself. All the great civilisations that have become extinct must have come to their end through some constant wrong expression of humanity; through slavery imposed upon fellow-beings; through parasitism on a gigantic scale bred by wealth, by man's clinging reliance on material resources; through a scoffing spirit of scepticism robbing us of our means of sustenance in the path of truth.

CONSCIOUSNESS is the light by the help v of which we travel along our path of life. But we cannot afford to squander this light at every step. Economy we need, and habit is that economy. It enables us to live and think without fully keeping our mind illumined. On festival nights we do not count the cost of our excess of light, because it is not for removing some deficiency, but for expressing the sense of our inner exuberance. And for the same reason habit becomes a sign of poverty in our spiritual life; for it is not a life of necessity, but of expression. In our love, our consciousness has to remain at its brightest, in order to be true. For love is no mere carrying out of some purpose, it is the full illumination of consciousness itself.

IF we allow our act of worship to deaden into a habit, then it frustrates itself, stiffening into mere piety which is a calculated economy of love. For worship has its worth, not in the action, but in a perfect outflow of consciousness in which habit has the tendency of becoming an impediment. We grow worldly in our devotion when we imagine that it confers upon us some special advantage, thus causing pious habits to be formed and valued. For when it is a question of profit, buying in the cheapest market is the best wisdom; but when complete giving out is the sole object, then economy is cheating one's own self.

THERE is one thing which is common in the process of the physical and the spiritual life. In both it is essential that we must forget the self. We know all the better what is around us by not having to remember our own selves at every step. When we are more to ourselves, then the world is less to us. But forgetfulness of self in our ordinary life of usefulness is mostly negative, it is attained by habit. Not so in the spiritual life, where self is forgotten because love is there. It is like the individual word, losing its meaning where it is separate, but regaining itself all the more where it is one with the whole poem. In the spiritual life we forget our exclusive individual purpose and are flooded with the spirit of perfection which through us transcends ourselves. In this we feel our immortality, which is the great meaning of our life.

OUR nature being complex, it is unsafe to generalise about things that are human; and it is an incomplete statement of truth to say that habits have the sole effect of deadening our mind. The habits that are helpful are like a channel, which helps the current to flow. It is open where the water runs onward, guarding it only where it has the danger of deviation. The bee's life in its channel of habit has no opening,--it revolves within a narrow circle of perfection. Man's life has its institutions which are its organised habits. When these act as enclosures, then the result may be perfect, like a beehive of wonderful precision of form, but unsuitable for the mind which has unlimited possibilities of growth.

FOR the current of our spiritual life creeds and rituals are channels that may thwart or help according to their fixity or openness. When a symbol of spiritual idea becomes rigidly elaborate in its construction, it supplants the idea which it should support. In art and literature metaphors which are the symbol of our emotional perceptions excite our imagination but do not arrest it. For they never claim a monopoly of our attention; they leave open the way for the endless possibility of other metaphors. They lose their artistic value if they degenerate into fixed habits of expression. Shelley, in his poem of the Skylark, pours out images which we value because they are only a few suggestions of the immeasurableness of our enjoyment. But if, because of their fitness and beauty, a law were passed that while thinking about a skylark these images should be treated as final and no others admitted, then Shelley's poem would at once become, false; for its truth is in its fluidity, in its modesty, which tacitly admits that it has not the last word.

THE other great body of ours is the world, with which this little body of ours ever aspires to establish a perfect relation of harmony. Is it simply for the sake of some convenience? Do our eyes try to see lest some danger or obstacle should come unawares in the dark, lest we might fail to find the things that are needful? No doubt these are powerful incentives, but the great fact lies in the delight of the meeting of our eyes with the world of lines, colours and movements. There is an incessant call from this universe of light, of sound, of touch, to our eyes, ears, to our limbs, and the response to it is a fulfilment which not only belongs to us, but to the great world. And this is the reason why from remote ages light incessantly knocked at the closed gates of life's blindness, till after repeated efforts life opened its windows of sight, and the union of the two was perfected. This was a wedding whose highest meaning is in its joy.

WE have a mental body, which has its organs of thought and feeling. There is the great social mind of man with which it seeks its harmony, for the perfecting of which experiments are carried on without rest. This aspiration also has not its source in expediency. It is an impulse for union which drives our mind across our little home and neighbourhood to its love tryst abroad. It must unite with the great mind of humanity to find its fulfilment. The beehive is the product of the truth of the unity in the bee's life; but literature, art and politics, moral laws and religions, which have no end to their freedom of growth, are born of the wedding of the man with Man.

THE question is asked, if life's journey be endless where is its goal? The answer is, it is everywhere. We are in a palace which has no end, but which we have reached. By exploring it and extending our relationship with it we are ever making it more and more our own. The infant is born in the same universe where lives the adult of ripe mind. But its position is not like a schoolboy who has yet to learn his alphabet, finding himself in a college class. The infant has its own joy of life because the world is not a mere road, but a home, of which it will have more and more as it grows up in wisdom. With our road the gain is at the end, but with this world of ours the gain is at every step; for it is the road and the home in one; it leads us on yet gives us shelter.

OUR life in the world is like listening to a song, to enjoy which we do not wait till it is finished. The song is there, in the singing from the very first note. Its unity permeates all its parts and therefore we do not impatiently seek the end, but follow the development. In the same way, because the world is truly one its parts do not tire us--only, our joy grows in depth with our deeper comprehension of its unity. At the moment when our various energies are employed with the varied in the world of nature and of man, the One in us is growing up towards the One in all. If the many and the one, the endless movement and the eternal reaching of the goal, were not in harmony in our being, our existence would be to us like ever learning grammar, and yet never coming to know any language.

NATURE is a mistress who tempts us with liberal wages--so much so, that we work extra hours for the extra remuneration. Yet in the midst of this bribery and these temptations man still cries for deliverance. For he knows that he is not a born slave and he refuses to be deluded into believing that to follow one's own desires unhindered is freedom. His real trust lies in his growth and not in his accumulations. The consciousness of a great inner truth lifts man from his surroundings of petty moments into the region of the eternal. It is the sense of something positive in himself for which he renounces his wealth, reputation, and life itself, and throws aside the scholar's book of logic, becoming simple as a child in his wisdom.

IN fact, man wants to reach that inner region where he can take his stand in the perfection of his unity, and not there where link upon link is forged, in an endless series, in the chain of things and events.

But as our body seeks its harmony with the great world-body for its fulfilment, so the one in us seeks its union with the great One. The One in us knows itself, has its delight in itself and expresses itself in its activities. It is truth and joy and expression. Therefore its union with the highest One must be in wisdom, in love and in service. This is our religion, that is to say, our higher nature. Its purposes cannot be definitely pointed out and explained, for it belongs to that life in the spiritual world where our objects have their recognition in something which we vaguely try to describe as blessedness,--a state of perfection, which is an end in itself. It is easy for man to ignore it and yet live, but man never did ignore it. He doubts it, mocks it, and strikes it, he fails in his realisation of it, but even in his failures and rebellions, in his desperate attempts to escape from it, he revolves round this one great truth.

A BLOCK of stone is unplastic, insensitive, inert, it offers resistance to the creative idea of the artist. But for a sculptor its very obstacles are an advantage and he carves his image out of it. Our physical existence is an obstacle to our spirit, it has every aspect of a bondage, and to all appearance it is a perpetual humiliation to our soul. And therefore it is the best material for our soul to manifest herself through it, to proclaim her freedom by fashioning her ornaments out of her fetters. The limitations of our outer circumstances are only to give opportunities to our soul, and by being able to defy them she realises her truth.

OUR living body in its relations to the physical world has its various wishes. These are to eat, to sleep, to keep warm or cool, as necessity demands--and many others. But it has one permanent wish, which is deeper and there-fore hidden. It is the wish for health. It works every moment fighting diseases and making constant adjustments with changing circumstances. The greater proportion of its activities are carried on behind our consciousness. He who has wisdom in regard to his physical welfare knows this and tries to establish harmony between the bodily desires that are conscious and this one desire which is latent. And he willingly sacrifices the claims of his appetites to the higher claim of his health.

We have our social body in which we come into relation with other men. Its obvious wishes are those that are connected with our selfish impulses. We want to get more than others and pay less than is our due. But there is another wish, deeply inherent in our social life, which is concerned with the welfare of the community. He who has social wisdom knows this and tries to bring all his clamorous wishes about personal pleasure, comfort and freedom under the dominion of this hidden wish for the good of others.

Likewise the obvious wish of our soul is to realise the distinction of its individuality, but it has its inherent wish to surrender itself in love to the Great Soul.

The wish for health takes into account the future of the body. The wish for the social good also has its outlook upon the time to come. They face the infinite. The wish of our soul to be one in love with the Great Soul transcends all limitations of time and space. Thus in our body, society, and soul we find on the surface the activity of numerous wishes and in their depth that of the one will which gives these wishes unity, leading them to peace, goodness, and love. In other words, on the one hand we have the wishes of the moment, and on the other the wish for the eternal. It is the function of our soul to unite these two and build its heaven upon the foundation of the earth.

A YOUNG friend of mine comes to me this morning to inform me that it is his birth-day and that he has just reached his nineteenth year. The distance between my age and his is great, and yet when I look at him it is not the incompleteness of his life which strikes me, but something which is complete in his youth. And in this differs the thing which grows, from the thing which is being made. A building in its unfinished stage is only too evidently unfinished. But in life's growth every stage has its perfection, the flower as well as the fruit.

WHEN I was a child, God also became a child with me to be my playmate. Otherwise my imperfections would have weighed me down, and every moment it would have been a misery to be and yet not fully to be. The things that kept me occupied were trifling and the things I played with were made of dust and sticks. But nevertheless my occupations were made precious to me and the importance that was given to my toys made them of equal value with the playthings of the adult. The majesty of childhood won for me the world's homage, because there was revealed the infinite in its aspect of the small.

And the reason is the same, which gives the youth the right to claim his full due and not to be despised. The divinity which is ever young, has crowned him with his own wreath, whispering to his ears that he is the rightful inheritor of all the world's wealth.

The infinite is with us in the beauty of our childhood, in the strength of our youth, in the wisdom of our age; in play, in earning, and in spending.

THE beauty which is in this evening sky comprehends forces tremendous in their awfulness. Yet it reveals to us the harmony which must be in the centre of all world activities, the harmony which has a still voice which is music itself. Because we are able to take view of this evening world where the distant and the near are brought face to face, we can see what is positively true in it--its beauty and unfathomable peace. When, through death, the deathlessness of some great life is discovered, the same vision of peace is revealed to us. The profound soul of Buddha is brought before our minds like this evening sky, and through all his struggles and sorrows, through his compassionate toil for men, we see a perfect assurance and repose of strength which is beauty. In smaller men the field of life is too narrow and therefore contra-dictions are too exaggerated to permit us any complete view of truth. But we may be sure, that in the currents of their lives as they run beyond death these contradictions are harmonised, for truth is over all, and beauty is the expression of truth.

IN the Upanishad God is described as "The Peaceful, the Good, the One." His peace is the peace of truth which we clearly see in Nature. The earth moves and the stars, every cell is moving and working in this tree, every blade of grass in this field is busy, and every atom of this evening star is restless, but peace is in the heart of all this movement--this movement which is creative. The movement which lacks this inner peace destroys. God, as the Peaceful, is revealed to him who has attained truth in his life, the truth which is ever active and yet which has an immensity of repose born of the mastery of self. It is not the loss of energy, the waning of life, which is peace, but their perfection.

An ignorant man finding himself in a factory for the first time in his life, is frightened at the bewildering medley of movements, but he who knows it is struck with admiration at the concentration of purpose dwelling in its centre, unmoved. This takes away all misgivings, and the perfect correlation of activities appears as beautiful. This is the peace which belongs to truth.

LIFE is a flow of harmony that united the in and the out, the end and the means, the what is and the what is to come. Life does not store up but assimilates, does not construct but creates, its work and itself are never dissociated. When the materials of our surroundings are not living, when they are fixed habits and hoarded possessions then our life and our world become separated and their mutual discord ends in the destruction of both. Or when some unbalanced excess of passion takes predominance in the buildings of our own world its distribution of weight goes wrong, and it constantly oppresses the wholeness of our life. The source of all the great evils in society, in government, in other organisations is in the alienation of the living being from its outer habitation. The gulf thus created by the receding stream of soul we try to replenish with a continuous pour of wealth which may have the power to fill but not the power to unite. Therefore the gap is dangerously concealed under glittering quicksands of things which by their own accumulating weight cause a sudden subsidence in the middle of our sleep of security.

THE world of senses in which animals live is limited. Our reason has opened the gate for our mind into the heart of the infinite. Yet this freedom of reason is but a freedom in the outer courtyard of existence. Objects of knowledge maintain an infinite distance from us who are the knowers. For knowledge is not union. Therefore the further world of freedom awaits us there where we reach truth, not through feeling it by senses or knowing it by reason, but through union of perfect sympathy. This is an emancipation difficult fully to imagine; we have but glimpses of its character. We perceive the fact of a picture by seeing it, we know about it by measuring its lines, analysing its colours and studying the laws of harmony in its composition. But even then it is no realisation of the picture, for which we want an intimate union with it immediate to ourselves.

THE picture of a flower in a botanical book is an information; its mission ends with our knowledge. But in pure art it is a personal communication. And therefore until it finds its harmony in the depth of our personality it misses its mark. We can treat existence solely as a text-book furnishing us lessons and we shall not be disappointed. But we know that there its mission does not end. For in our joy in it which is an end in itself we feel that it is a communication, the final response to which is not the response of our knowing but the response of our being.

WHEN Buddha preached *Maitri*--the relationship of harmony--not only with human beings but with all creation, did he not have this truth in his mind that our treatment of the world is wrong when we solely treat it as a fact which can be known and used? Did he not feel that its meaning can be attained only through love because it is an expression of love which waits for its answer from our soul emancipated from the bondage of self? This emancipation cannot be negative in character, for love can never lead to negation. The perfect freedom is in a perfect harmony of relationship and not in a mere severance of bondage. Freedom has no content, and therefore no meaning, where it has nothing but itself. Soul's emancipation is in the fulfilment of its relation to the central truth of everything that there is, which is impossible to define because it is in the end of all definitions.

NO flame burns for ever. Light goes out for want of oil, is puffed out by the wind, often the lamp itself is shattered. In our fit of irritation we may say that the power of darkness is final and true, or that we create light ourselves by lighting the lamp. But the truth is that every extinction of light is to prove that the source of light is without end, and man's true power lies only in his ability to prove this over and over again.

I BELIEVE that there is an ideal hovering over and permeating the earth,-- an ideal of that Paradise which is not the mere outcome of fancy, but the ultimate reality in which all things are and towards which all things are moving. I believe that this vision of Paradise is to be seen in the sunlight, and the green of the earth, in the flowing streams, in the gladness of springtime, the repose of a winter morning, in the beauty of human face and wealth of human love. Everywhere in this earth the spirit of Paradise is awake and sending forth its voice. It reaches our inner ears without our knowing it. It tunes our harp of life, urging us to send our aspiration beyond the finite, as flowers send their perfume into the air and birds their songs.

OUR energies are employed in supplying ourselves with things and plea- sures. They have no eternity in their background. There-fore we try to give things an appearance of permanence by making them big. Man in his anxiety to prolong his pleasure and power tries to make additions, and we are afraid to stop, because we fear that they must some day come to an end.

But truth is not afraid to be small, to come to an end,--just as a poem, when it is finished, is not really dead. Not because a poem is composed of endless lines but because it carries an ideal of perfection. The pauses of truth has the cadence of the infinite, its disappearances are the processional arches on its path of immortality.

WE light the lamp in our room which creates a seeming opposition be- tween it and the great outside world. Our life on the earth is like that small room in which our consciousness has been concentrated. And we imagine that outside it lies death which opposes it. But the one indivisible truth of existence which is for us must not be doubted because our life obscures it for a moment.

THE vision of life which we see in the world is a vision of joy. The joy is in its ever flowing colour, music and dance. If there were truth in death this spir- it of joy would vanish from the heart of existence. The lamp we light in the night has a wick which is small and oil which is very little. But there is no timidness in its tiny flame burning as it is in the heart of an immense darkness; for the truth of the light which sustains it is infinite.

THE world, like a stream of sounds in music, is a perpetual flow of forces and forms, and therefore from the outside it has an aspect of impermanence. There it represents death, being a continual current of losses. But the loss is only for the channel, the instrument through which music is made to pass. It is the unity of melody which ever survives the fleeting notes. If individual notes could claim a pro-longed endlessness then they would miss their true eternity which is the music. The desert has the quality of the immutable because it lacks life. In a soil which is fruitful, life reveals its immortality by its ceaseless passage through death.

IT is given to us to reveal our soul, that which is One in us, which is eternal. This can only be done by its passage through the fleeting Many; to assert the infinity of the spirit by continual sacrifice of forms. The self being the vessel that gathers and holds gives us the opportunity of giving up. If we believe only in self then we anxiously cling to our stores which causes us misery and failure. When we believe in soul the very inconstancy of life finds its eternal meaning and we feel that we can afford to lose.

Lector House believes that a society develops through a two-fold approach of continuous learning and adaptation, which is derived from the study of classic literary works spread across the historic timeline of literature records. Therefore, we aim at reviving, repairing and redeveloping all those inaccessible or damaged but historically as well as culturally important literature across subjects so that the future generations may have an opportunity to study and learn from past works to embark upon a journey of creating a better future.

This book is a result of an effort made by Lector House towards making a contribution to the preservation and repair of original ancient works which might hold historical significance to the approach of continuous learning across subjects.

HAPPY READING & LEARNING!

LECTOR HOUSE LLP
E-MAIL: lectorpublishing@gmail.com